For more information, please contact information@thejoyfactorbook.com or visit thejoyfactorbook.com.

Cover art by Wren Roger.
Cover design by Shelly Turner.

Printed in the USA.
Published by Aspire Books
aspirebooks.org.

ISBN 978-1-7342893-5-0

Lisa Roger

The Joy Factor

Escaping Job Disappointment
and Finding Your Dream Career

**Aspire
Books**

aspirebooks.org

Karri,

All the best
with your journey

To my two beautiful children, who are
starting their adult journey.

To my love Scott who pushed
me to write it all down.

And to my family that has followed
their joy, provided great examples of
taking calculated risks, and embodied
the American Dream.

Table of Contents

List of Figures

Acknowledgements

I would like to take this opportunity to thank the many people who have encouraged and supported this journey. Scott Kamp, my soulmate, listened to hundreds of my stories over the years and persuaded me to write it all down, and to share my stories about self-discovery and happiness.

My beautiful Wren, first born, designed and illustrated the original version of the cover of this book.

My niece, Ashleigh Clokey, the closest millennial to me that I know, read the book out loud, so I could hear the story in the voice of the people I most hope to help and inspire.

My editor, Cleis Abeni, and my designer, Shelly Turner, helped direct me to the finish line.

Then there are those who were there in the trenches with me: leaders, cohorts, peers, and mentors, who you will meet in the stories in this book. The Fabulous Five, including Cynthia Shelton, took a chance on a Stay-at-Home Mom and opened a world of possibilities.

Although barely mentioned here, my parents are powerful role models: they provided me a university of examples of effective practices for business, leadership, and risk-taking. I'm grateful for their love and support.

Foreword

....

Thank you for taking the time to read my thoughts on finding that perfect position that will bring you fulfillment, satisfaction, financial well-being, and peace. This book attempts to provide a roadmap and a strategy to find your career passion. This book is about finding joy, happiness, and success in your career.

I share personal stories that highlight my success in finding the ultimate position that I love, and I also describe the bumps along the way in my career. I provide exercises to help you with your personal journey of self-discovery. You can use these exercises are references whenever you are about to take on a new position, pursue promotion, or navigate a job search. Regardless of the career change, you can take the time to review the exercises to help guide you pick the best path.

I decided to write this book about ten years ago, but I didn't fully commit until I made a vital discovery: the method that I share here not only worked for me, but for my friends, colleagues, and the young professionals that I had the privilege to mentor. The Joy Factor is a decision-making method that helps you have effective conversations around professional and personal development.

My personal journey is like many other people's experiences. I hated my first job. The consistent daily pain and frustration of that experience became a catalyst for change: my disillusionment drove me to do something—to change my career outlook. I had to hone in and locate my power to be happy. I found the essential ingredients—the joy factor—that epitomized that power and now I share that method of empowerment with you.

This book has nine short chapters composed like sparks to stimulate insight and encourage action. I frame the chapters with a Foreword and an Afterword that share how and why my message benefits you. I often talk about marshaling power in this book, including embracing our power of gratitude.

So, as you embark on this journey of discovery, I say, "Be empowered" and may all your best hopes be realized.

Chapter 1

Not Deciding

Finding job satisfaction; discovering your passion in life—these things don't always hit you like a strike of lightning. There are always people who know exactly what they want to do with their lives. They went to school and studied their craft until they were accomplished enough to live their dreams. Even the pursuit— the process of learning to attain their goal—is fulfilling to them, inspiring momentum to drive forward, to pull through, and complete their training so that they might live out their goals.

These people are the lucky

ones. They live their dreams. They find the right positions. They live in the life that they want. But, most of us are not so lucky. For the rest of us, we need an approach that will help us navigate the difficulties, indecisions, and setbacks that typify the challenges of finding our ideal careers.

In college, I met dorm mates and friends who knew exactly what they wanted to be: nurses, accountants, lawyers, and artists. But, I had no idea. I remember attending orientation. We were in a very large auditorium with all the other incoming college freshmen and their parents. My father sat next to me and we filled out forms (this was before the Internet). I looked at the blank next to the section pertaining to what my major would be. I didn't know what to write on the form. My father told me to choose Management Information Systems. He said that I could start there and change once I discovered what I wanted to do later in my life.

Yet, throughout my college experience, I never discovered what I wanted to do. I remember enjoying accounting and finance and, at one point, I seriously considered changing majors. Then I learned how competitive accounting was and that you had to have perfect grades in math, including calculus and statistics, to be considered for any of the positions with the big eight accounting firms. I never changed the major that my dad selected for me that fateful day in the auditorium.

I envied my friends, who just seemed to know where they were going and how they would get there. I also wondered if I was the only one "not deciding." I stayed the course to get through, but I did not really commit to a calling. In fact, I had no idea what my calling was let alone how to commit to it.

Later in life, I learned that most people were just like me. We aren't all born with an innate awareness that guides us to the finish line of a career. We don't know our passion and the roadmap to get there on the day we graduate from high school. We must figure it out and it's not easy.

The truth is, only you can define your roadmap—not our parents, guidance counselors, an aptitude test, or a psychic. It is not your employer's responsibility to define your path, and nor is it your supervisor's. It's your job to find your way to happiness. The journey to find yourself is a deeply personal one that requires having honest conversations with yourself and deep introspection. The good news is this: if you purposefully focus and put energy into the process, it really is not as difficult as it seems.

For me, I stumbled through my college experience, gained my degree, and my first job without knowing if I was going to like information systems or not. I was "not deciding" and I had not committed to a process. I knew then that I didn't like programming. Not only did I not like it, I also wasn't good at it. I remember enjoying the courses that addressed more business-related topics like marketing and management. Even then, there were indicators of the things that I genuinely enjoyed that foreshadowed what would later become my future career.

Summary

How do we navigate through our careers and get to that destined end state? We must understand that not everyone is lucky enough to know their calling early. Most of us do not have that clarity in the beginning. That's okay. It's normal. There is a sense of unrest, dissatisfaction, and discontent that comes strongly at the beginning of the journey. That is the universe letting you know that you are not firing on all cylinders. Start your discovery process early so that you can confront the seemingly endless toil of unrewarding employment.

Chapter 2

Rough but Resilient

From the year my father and I sat in the auditorium at orientation when I first entered college until today, the career prospects and employment security of United States citizens has dimmed. For most of this book, I discuss the power that we have within ourselves to find a joyful career. But, I would like to pause for a few moments to consider the societal factors that have made finding a joyful career challenging for many of us. I hope that understanding these factors can make us even more resilient as we find The Joy Factor that will allow us to overcome societal obstacles and find individual success.

Despite relatively low unemployment, and the strongest labor market in half a century, many Americans still struggle to find employment, especially after losing a job. On Halloween day in 2019, The New York Times highlighted the story of a woman named Laura Ward.

"After more than a decade as production manager at a small advertising agency, Ms. Ward was let go after the firm lost a major account," Patricia Cohen reported in the article. "Over the last three and a half years, she has worked temporary stints, and bolstered her skills by taking a project-management course at a nearby college. But she has not been able to find a steady, full-time job. So for her, the reports of low unemployment rates and employer complaints of labor shortages are puzzling."

Laura lives in New Jersey within, as the article noted, commuting distance of New York City, an area with seemingly high job prospects within her field, yet she still struggled to find full-time employment with a strong income, benefits, and job security. Laura has become part of the "gig economy": the large number of Americans who work temporary jobs to stay afloat. Working just one hour on a job removes an individual from the statistics that track unemployment. Thus, today's unemployment rate of 3.6 percent (as of October 2019) hides the millions of Americans who are temporary workers.

"There are also many others,

like Ms. Ward, who work temporary jobs for months at a time and are not necessarily captured in [statistics]," notes The New York Times article. "And millions of contract workers—freelancers, consultants, Lyft drivers—lack benefits, regular schedules, and job security. They have found a foothold, but it rests on loose rock."

The "loose rock" of unemployment has certainly come from a succession of economic recessions and depressions, be they the tech bust at the turn of the 21st century or the severe depression in 2008 when major banks were bailed out by the U.S. government while homeowners and people with student debt were not.

Speaking of student debt, imagine this predicament: a four-year college degree has become a de facto requirement for even entry-level positions in most fields. But the cost of a college education, including at public institutions, has skyrocketed to the point where the neediest low-income students and middle class individuals struggle to pay for tuition. Consequently, many people take out exorbitant loans, making student debt in higher education a bona fide national crisis.

"As many as 44.7 million Americans have student loan debt, according to a 2018 report by the Federal Reserve Bank of New York," said Nigel Chiwaya in a NBC News report from April 24, 2019. "The total amount of student loan debt is $1.47 trillion as of the end of 2018: more than credit cards or auto loans."

The most alarming problem of the student loan crisis is that the jobs that individuals find (whether temporary, part-time, or full-time) often do not command the kind of robust salaries that allow individuals to successfully retire their student loan debt.

Moreover, Americans face an employment terrain full of diminishing industries that once sustained us. Ten years into the 21st century, newspapers across the country warned of a "retail apocalypse." Once beloved brick and mortar retail chains like Sears went belly up and even the ubiquitous dollar stores struggle to stay fiscally afloat.

Walmart, Inc. is one of the rare winner among physical retail stores and Amazon is one of the biggest success stories in online retail.

Yet, arguably, working for both of these retailers rarely provides middle class wages, benefits, and job security for most of these companies' workers, and some pundits have called these trends the "death of the middle class."

In 2018, it did not seem surprising when G.M. closed plants and laid off thousands of workers. Skilled factory employment has long been in decline and the good wages, benefits, and job security that Americans in this form of employment enjoyed at the middle of the 20th century seems mostly to be the hallmark of a bygone era. Many of these skilled factory jobs were union jobs.

In a February 1, 2018 report, The New York Times cited six reasons why "pay has lagged behind

U.S. job growth":

1. Declining Unionization;
2. Restraints on Competition;
3. A Lagging Minimum Wage;
4. Globalization and Automation;
5. Sluggish Productivity;
6. Outsourcing.

The gig economy has produced a veritable army of contractors. Union membership is down while employment is increasingly concentrated into a handful of multinational corporations. Many of these corporations have moved significant portions of their business our of the U.S. where they pay workers in other countries significantly less with few benefits. In consideration of the high cost of living, it is increasingly absurd that the "federal minimum wage, currently $7.25 an hour, has not increased since 2009, and its purchasing power has never returned on a sustained basis to what it delivered in the 1960s and '70s," as The New York Times article on pay stagnation explained.

"As job losses soar and the media continues to report on falling stock prices and rising foreclosures, many people may react to the economic climate with a flood of strong emotions and a sense of uncertainty. Yet, people generally adapt well over time to life-changing situations and stressful conditions," said a special report by the American Psychological Association entitled "Staying Resilient Through Tough Economic Times."

"What helps some people

'bounce back' while others continue to feel overwhelmed? Resilience, the process of adapting well in the face of adversity," and principles and practices that comprise The Joy Factor in this book are nothing short of a recipe for resilience in troubling economic times. Regardless of societal challenges, it is still possible to structure our mindset to find happiness in what we do. There is a special power in rising to fight the good fight, and my aim in this book is to show you how honing our resilience makes all the difference in the world.

Summary

While societal trends make maintaining and finding employment challenging; and while finding and funding credentials, training, and

education are increasingly difficult; neither of these obstacles can
disadvantage us if we accentuate
the positive and stay resilient. The
method shared in this book guides
you to operationalize resilience by
focusing on what brings you joy in
your career. No amount of money
can supplant the capturing of this
joy in one's working life and all the
obstacles in the world are no match
for an uplifting frame of mind when
keeping and seeking employment.

Chapter 3

The Joy Factor

So how do you do it already?! For those of you who skipped straight to this chapter, I don't blame you. I have read one thousand diet books and I always go straight to the food list to see if I can do it or if it is worth the energy to read the newest craze. When you reach my stage in your career you should love 80 to 100 percent of what you do: that is The Joy Factor. This method is about making the right decisions to get you there.

I will be honest with you: in the beginning your first choices for your career may be disappointing. I know mine were. For over 30 years, I've watched college graduates come into the work force and seen the life being sucked out of them as they come to understand the reality of their jobs.

You may be thinking, "Yes, my job sucks, I hate my cubicle, and the work I am given is mind numbingly boring. I can't possibly move myself to be grateful for this position. I wanted to make a difference, to be valued and to change the world. How can I do that from where I am today, when I see absolutely no sign of opportunity to do any of that?"

Even more difficult is the situation where you have a terrible boss or co-worker that creates an environment where you are miserable. Even in this most difficult example, finding joy is a responsibility you owe to yourself.

When you are in that dreadful job and experience daily misery, at a minimum you are going to learn what you do NOT want to do, but I would bet that you can admit that there are a few things that you might like to do too. Be aware, take note, and observe.

Exercise: For the next two weeks keep two lists. At lunch, during a break and at the end of the day, take time to record what you loved doing throughout the day and what you hated doing. Things you record should include interactions with people: describe what you liked or disliked about the exchange. What were you doing in your work? Giving advice, problem solving, gossiping, or networking? Think about the meetings you attend, which ones do you look forward to during the week? Why? Here is a hypothetical example for these two lists to use for our discussion.

Figure 1

Joy Tasks	Negative Tasks
Mentoring others	Approving requisitions
Coaching a team through a difficult problem	Telling someone they need to improve their work products
Productive meetings	Super long meetings where nothing was decided
Winning a proposal	Organizing your desk
Proofreading others' work	Writing that first paragraph of a long executive summary
Motivating others to take on something new	Running out of things to do

Notice what you have recorded. Which list is longer? The goal is to have the joy side stretch longer than the negative. Take the lists and see if you can categorize or group the similar items. You should see some patterns. Are there items in the negative column that you can control to squeeze out something positive? The next step is to evaluate how much time do you spend on each element. Recording a percentage is probably the easiest approach. Just make sure that it adds up to 100 percent!

Figure 2

Joy Tasks	Negative Tasks
Mentoring others 10%	Approving requisitions 3%
Coaching a team through a difficult problem 20%	Telling someone they need to improve their work products 5%
Productive meetings 20%	Super long meetings where nothing was decided 5%
Winning a proposal 10%	Organizing your desk 2%
Proofreading others' work 5%	Writing that first paragraph of a long executive summary 3%
Motivating others to take on something new 15%	Running out of things to do 2%

Figure 3

Joy Assessment

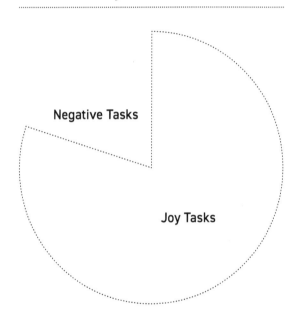

When it's time to take a new position or role, don't look for a bigger title, more money, or a better commute. These are the three fatal flaws of career development. Look for the next position that allows you to spend more of your day in the joy column. No matter what choice you make, do not choose a position where The Joy Factor is less. In the interview process, imagine the time when they ask, "Do you have any questions?" You should now be armed with many! Ask about expectations pertaining to your joy, such as, "Will you have more opportunities there?"

Be careful not to whine when investigating the negative requirements. Ask open-ended questions to pinpoint what you love or disdain. "Please describe how you would envision my role in [X] and what other resources or team members participate in the process and what are their responsibilities?" might be one of your questions. Your goal is to discover how much of your joy list will be manifest in the job for which you are interviewing.

This exercise of writing down what is important to you is key for the next steps. It may also be fun to do. The next step is to expand on this assignment and look at past positions. Go back to each role you can remember and do your best to document what you loved and hated. Now you have a more robust picture of what has given you joy. Now we will take this to the next level and think about the "why."

We need to expand that journal and evolve it into a log focused on your career journey. In the journal keep a record of what you learned about your personal joy. The list you created above will feed this table. What was the title of the position? In a few bullets, what were the positive elements of the role? Also write down the negative parts. Most importantly take time to write down what you learned from this position? Try to only record the learning that was positive. I know it will not always be possible, but it will be more powerful if you can stick to the positive. If I were journaling in this manner about my first employment positions, then my journal would look something like the following illustration.

Figure 4

Position	Positives	Negatives	Lessons
C++ Maintenance Programmer	The win in solving the bugs, talking to the end users, sharing what I learned	Solitude, working alone, staring at someone else's code, the wins are too far apart	I like to solve hard problems, be with people, I don't have the patience to figure out programming problems
Sign Language Interpreter	Being the center of attention, learning how to own a business, the challenge of learning a new language and culture	Interpreters cannot give their opinion; they can't solve problems when they are interpreting	I love the attention, the challenge of learning something new and the business elements, but I also love to give my opinion
Technical Trainer	Being the center of attention, public speaking, helping others learn	Teach the same thing over and over	I still love the attention, but I do not like doing the same thing everyday, repetition
ISP Co-Owner	Loved setting up the business, watching the business grow, accounts receivable, budgeting, marketing	Losing bids, solitude	I learned that I loved finance and business growth and marketing, I enjoy an office with more people than less

At my first position after college, I decided that I desperately wanted to have a job where I was adding value and being valued. I still didn't know what I wanted to do. Several years into the role, I still was unhappy and unfulfilled. But, there were some things that I learned.

The beginning of my career journey had a major sidetrack. I love to share this story and I'm sure there are parts to which you can relate. I was in a cubicle that had no windows and a combination lock to get in and out of the room. I was doing maintenance programming, which basically means I would get discrepancy reports and need to research through someone else's code (that was not documented) to try and find out why the program was not working as expected. Admittedly, I was not the best programmer. In college, rather than advancing in the CO-BOL programming classes, I excelled at business analysis, management, marketing, and communication courses.

So here I was not doing any of the subjects that I liked—only the ones I hated!

The most interesting part of my day was when I got the opportunity to talk with my customer. He was deaf. My customer hired sign language interpreters to help with communication, interpreting meetings and giving sign language classes to the team. I had already learned how to sign my ABCs as a kid watching Sesame Street! This was the highlight of my week! I would practice and my customer would take time to teach me new signs so I wouldn't have to spell every word. I started to get pretty good at it. I also became friends with the sign language interpreters and learned about their job. I was soaking it all in. It was my escape from programming. I started to come in each day with a list of ten words I wanted to learn. I would either learn them from my customer or the interpreter. My vocabulary was growing every day. I was getting better.

Then one fateful day the interpreter couldn't make a major meeting. I was asked to sit in and interpret the meeting. I was thrilled to have the opportunity and I loved it! The customer and his boss noticed how well I performed. I remember that meeting like it was yesterday. The meeting was over and the Branch Chief (my customer's boss) pulled me aside and let me know he was impressed with my abilities. They felt I was so good that they sent me to Gallaudet University, the famous university for the deaf, and paid for classes to hone my skills.

As the months passed I did more and more interpreting and less and less programming. At one point, I went to my current employer and asked that they change the contract and let me interpret instead of programming. I explained that the customer had faith in my abilities and would support the change. I explained that the going rate for interpreters was much higher than the junior programming rate I was earning then. Plus, I had a technical background that the other interpreters didn't have. This would be a win-win for everyone involved. My company turned down the proposal and said that it was too far out of scope. They didn't understand the role, or the risks involved and were not willing to learn.

I left to start my own company. I was interpreting technical topics and that brought technology into the joy column for me. I was escaping from the parts I hated and learning something new. My joy list was so long during that transition. This was the first time I discovered how much I enjoyed being the center of attention. I also loved the business side of owning my own company. I like the finances and the independence of setting up my own limited liability corporation (LLC). I needed to discover many things and that journey heightened The Joy Factor.

Back to the journal: one of the

other things you may have noticed is that I took a negative element and reframed it as a positive factor. Under the interpreting example, ethically an interpreter must never get involved in a conversation. That may seem counterintuitive, but an interpreter's role is to convey the message in a way that respects the spirit in which it is given. One of the most frustrating experiences in that role is when two individuals are try-ing to negotiate, compromise, and problem solve and you can see the "answer," yet you are not a partic-ipant in the conversation. The two people need to come to solutions on their own, and you really are a machine in many ways.

In journaling, when you look at my list, you will see that, instead of highlighting that I didn't like not being included in the conversation and not giving my opinion, I reframed this example and stated that I enjoy problem solving. Both statements are true, but the second one has a positive twist. Again, envision yourself in an interview process. How do you convey that you don't want to do something by highlighting the part that you do enjoy? It may seem like a subtle shift, but I guarantee you that this shift is powerful.

Summary

Start by noticing and documenting the daily tasks and interactions that you enjoy. Keep that list of negative tasks that drain the energy from you. Maintain that list for several weeks, until you feel confident that you have captured your current role and all that it offers you. During this time, you can also begin looking back at all your past positions and make a very robust set of lists to carry over into the next exercise.

Create your career journal. Summarize each position that you have had and identify the positive and negative elements. Pinpoint what you have learned about your joy factors. Make a concerted effort when documenting the lessons learned to state them in a positive way.

These steps are the building blocks in creating your roadmap to that perfect position. You can use this roadmap or list of requirements, to not only help you discover and bring into focus what you love, but also to help you as you transition into new roles.

Again, use this approach as you search for a job, when you acquire a job, and during transition times between jobs. Doing these things will help you clearly articulate what is important and what you are expecting in your next role.

Chapter 4

The Broken Handle

....

The journey to joy in a career is attainable. There are frames of mind that will help you along the way. Chief among these frames is to always be grateful for all opportunities. No matter what position you are in, no matter what strain issues from your boss is, you must try to remain positive. Too often we focus on the negative or what we don't want.

Being positive also involves acknowledging the aspects of your current life that you enjoy. Ask yourself questions like this: what can you learn, what can be gained, and how can you add value to your employment experiences? Changing your frame of mind requires tools. I recommend four foundational actions that will help you in your journey towards joy in your career:

1. Keep a gratitude journal;
2. Find an anchor;
3. Conserve your energy; and
4. Avoid negativity.

Keep a Gratitude Journal

Some of the hardest and most unrewarding times in my life were softened when I tapped into the power of a gratitude journal. I survived by this seemingly simple exercise. This exercise involves recording daily the things that go well professionally and personally to elevate the value of our experiences.

When applied specifically to your job, or the people you work with, keeping a gratitude journal will shift your perception and shift your interpretation of your circumstances. More importantly, it presents a road map for finding positivity in your life, and it defines what you can become as you create positivity for yourself.

Use whatever method makes you comfortable: keep the gratitude journal on your computer; or keep it in a handwritten fancy bounded book like the ones that you purchase from the gift card shop. As you write, ask yourself the following questions:

- What happened today that you are grateful for?
- What exchange with another human being makes me grate-

ful—was it something that they or I did that helped or supported us, or was it just a simple laugh shared together?

- How can I train my brain to notice even the smallest incidents and experiences that warm my heart?

There are some days that are so bad that I think there is absolutely nothing for which I can be grateful. Then I remember coming home and getting warm welcomes and dog hugs from my fur babies. Or I remember noticing nature: there is so much to appreciate there—what blooms in my flowerbeds? In the spring, I look into the woods and search for flowering dogwoods. Joy is easy to find and becoming grateful for the joy will reframe your thinking.

Find An Anchor

Another effective tool I use is to have an anchor. An anchor is a physical object that you can touch and see. Typically, it is portable, meaning, you can take it with you anywhere that you travel. There is a lot of literature about having an anchor. For some it is a religious symbol, as it is in some Christian cultures where the most well known anchor is the cross.

I personally have a very strong anchor that reminds me of a particularly difficult but rewarding time in my life. I was raising two young kids in Texas and my husband had lost his job, again. This was during the Dot-com bubble crash in the late 1990's. For around six years we struggled with being employed and then being laid off. We made a science out of being frugal. How many meals could we get out of one whole chicken? We watered down hand soap, mended clothes, attended free concerts in the park, and accepted offers for dinner from neighbors. We survived on eBay, selling everything from used clothes to our wedding china. I scoured yard sales and bought all the denim that I could to then resell it on eBay. We had yard sales and cleaned other peoples' houses. I learned how to use the bread pantries to get enough carbohydrates for a few bucks that lasted two weeks to feed my family.

Even during this hardship, there was joy to be found. When I took my kids to the pantry, we selected staples like bread, tortillas, and chips. If we purchased $6 worth of product, we could pick two individually wrapped Hostess pies. My kids picked the flavors they wanted, and apple was the winning flavor on most visits. They were so happy, sugared up, and sticky by the time we got home. In this dark time when treats were rare, those inexpensive Hostess pies were something I was grateful for...

During this tough time, I was able to get a job at a local community center. I was hired as the assistant manager to help run their re-sale shop. We would take donations from the community, clean them and sometimes fix them up and then re-sell the items in our storefront. One of the benefits of the position was that employees could purchase any donated items for 25¢ apiece. I took advantage of this benefit often to get new clothes for the kids and household items for myself.

One day this beautiful briefcase came in. It was two-tone dark
in light leather and a monogram
with EWR on the front. My mar-
ried name is Elese Roger and my
maiden name is Walker, so I thought
wow this was meant to be mine.
The only issue with the brief case
was the handle was cracked. It was
a deep crack, almost split in two,
but connected with a strip of leather
on the inside. It was beautiful, but
we couldn't sell it, as it was broken,
and we couldn't mend the leather.
I bought it thinking that one day
when I went back to my true calling
and career, I would use this case.
In my eyes, it was beautiful and
unique. Somehow, I was meant to
have it.

Fast forward many years later

and I used that briefcase, every day, and I loved it. At my first position after coming back from being a stay-at-home Mom, I was rising up the ranks. Within nine months, I was selected to be the program manager in one of the largest divisions at my company. A year later, my team won a series of awards including "program of the year" and I personally won an award for leading large programs, a huge honor.

"You can go have that handle fixed," I remember one of my staff members telling me soon after receiving the award. They commented on how the satchel was such a beautiful case and that I should go get it fixed so it will be perfect. It was then that I realized how that case with the broken handle was my anchor. It was an albeit imperfect, physical emblem that kept hope and opportunity alive for me each that I went to work.

The case reminded me everyday of the time when I was sorting through donations just to feed my family. It was a daily reminder of my struggle and where I had come from. Holding the handle and feeling in the heel of my hand on the break, the stiffness of the leather and the softer center of the break. It reminded me of my own strength and what I was able to endure. My current role, although prestigious, was really no test to the internal strength that was required to survive and provide for my family.

I can bring back that feeling of strength in my brain. It was not only a memory of overcoming something; it was also a feeling that brings a sense of comfort. At the same time, it is a reminder that I made it through that time, and I have the confidence to tackle almost anything.

I now use a laptop case versus a briefcase, but I have my briefcase predominately displayed in my closet, so I'm reminded every day. It helps ground me. It reminds me to be grateful for the opportunity that I enjoy and not to take for granted my circumstances. Again, I can recall what it felt like to have that handle in my hand. I don't need that daily interaction, and its strength is now a part of who I am.

Here is an exercise that you may find indispensable. Take stock of your life. What has had meaning or impact? Religion, a person, a country or a sports team that inspires you? Was there an event, a win, or a meaningful experience that is personal and unique? The more emotion associated with the anchor, the better. Make a list of all these events/items/people. You might struggle to come up with one example or you may have a robust list.

Once you have a good list, analyze what you have documented. Make sure that you can draw positive energy from the entry. If you can't then delete that item from the list. A divorce, death of a loved one, being fired—all are emotional experiences, but if they didn't leave you with emotional strength as their outcomes, then remove them from the list. On the other hand, a struggle that left you resilient or stronger is an excellent example.

Once you have narrowed

down your list, think of something tangible that represents the item. Lucky penny, rabbit's foot, rubbing stones, and a cross are all traditional examples of anchors. If the event has no symbol, you can make one. Several years ago, there was a movement where people bought special stones to represent positivity and gratefulness. Taking a smooth stone and decorating it with a marker can do the trick.

Now that you have your anchor, use it. Again, it needs to be an item that you will be forced to "interact" with several times a day.

Conserve Your Energy

Being grateful, acknowledging the positive experiences, and making the most of every day life will take you very far. These actions will help you conserve your energy so you can be strong to overcome obstacles when it matters the most. Even when I was working at the re-sale shop, I enjoyed engaging with customers. It seemed as if I was accomplishing impossible tasks but I thrived when mentoring the court-appointed "volunteers" who came to work at the shop.

It is easy to sometimes feel sorry for yourself, but you never need to expend that kind of energy. You may feel that your current role is not your career path but no matter the role you have there is an opportunity to learn, observe, and build towards your dreams.

If you can't attune your energy to recognize your current joy, it is almost impossible to move forward. Daily acknowledgement and development of a centered, balanced sense of energy will help you move forward.

Avoid Negativity

Buffering your mind with negativity can be like a drug. It is a form of entertainment that is very addicting. It is even more enticing if you have a circle of friends that like to share in that form of entertainment. I'm sure you know the group that hangs out at the water cooler and can't wait to pick apart the latest move by the boss. Getting caught up in this environment will be a death trap and a non-starter in finding your joy. When I was miserable in my career, I found this circle of negativity very comforting.

It is very difficult to extricate oneself from the circle of doom. It almost is impossible. I would say, losing weight would be on the same level of difficulty. There is an adrenaline rush that comes with pointing out the negative. To get yourself out of this trap takes practice and awareness. You need to notice that you are doing it and redirect your thinking. Redirect your negative thinking to a positive frame of mind.

The next time you are faced with the opportunity to opine about the next injustice, physically remove yourself from that environment. Make an excuse, like, "I have to go to the bathroom" or "I'm late for a meeting." Then when you are back at your desk, re-examine the assumed crime. Was it really that negative? Could there be information that you are not aware of that is driving the issue? If the situation is one where you had a personal exchange with a co-worker, it is an even better opportunity for reframing your thinking. If you had a fight or disagreement with someone and you are thinking they are so stubborn, or stupid, or old fashioned (you can fill in the blank), then you should re-examine the situation. There is only one element in this exchange that you can control and that is yourself. So, were you listening? Do you really understand where that person is coming from? Can you put yourself in their shoes?

Each of these situations may make you uncomfortable. You recognize the feeling. When you are in that place, take a second and understand that this is an opportunity for growth as you change the negative to the positive. Look for the win.

It is all in your frame of mind. So, you should make a habit of creating joyful situations. Look for opportunities to highlight the positive, drop a compliment or do someone a favor. When you get home at night and you get that time of night to share your day with someone, start it off with something that happened that was positive.

I recently took on a position leading an IT organization. One of my leads came to let me know that he was trying to get the organization to invest in a solution for many years, but they would never approve the expense. He said, but I know you will go in there all full of energy and positivity and they won't be able to deny the proposal. He was right. We got the support. People like saying, "Yes," to positive people.

If you enter a challenge with a bundle of nerves, then you may be defeating yourself. In contrast if you enter with a challenge assuming a positive outcome, the stress will be less, and your positive energy will impact the session in a good way. I like to enter with a smile on my face and be genuinely excited about my topic and how I know that what I am briefing will bring about positive change to the organization. Confidence goes a long way, and if you genuinely believe in what you're selling, your confidence will accentuate the positive!

Summary

Essentially, the four actions recommended in this chapter are about

having the right frame of mind.
There is a level of anxiety one experiences, when you dwell in negativity. The power of changing your
frame of mind is an enduring action
that was even represented in Napoleon Hill's classic 1928 book, *The
Law of Success*. Keep a gratitude
journal. Find an anchor. Conserve
your energy. Avoid negativity. When
your days are surrounded with positive energy, it will come back to you
and you will benefit from it in ways
you can't even imagine.

Chapter 5

Lead Singer
for ABBA

······

What you find joy in today may not
be the same tomorrow. There are
often core factors that will remain
consistent throughout your life,
and you will need to maintain those
factors and discard others that are
no longer adding value to your joy. I
often wonder if the passion remains
the same for those who choose a
calling when they were teenagers,
obtain training, and work within
their chosen careers. I imagine it
would be difficult to try something
different after all that investment.

This almost makes my "non-decisive" approach a bit more palatable.

Think back to your childhood when you wanted to be in a rock band. Okay, that was me. I thought I could really be the lead singer of ABBA even though I couldn't hold a tune. Whatever your dream position was—fireman, teacher, astronaut, doctor, lawyer, etc.—it held your imagination at that time. Why did those careers no longer hold your attention when were in college? You may have discovered that they required a strength or attribute you didn't have, or were not willing to learn/earn, or that you changed your mind.

Whatever the catalyst, the point is that you changed. As you move through your career, you may find that your new position is the job of your dreams. You will have a sense of contentment. Well, I am here to tell you that the position will most likely lose its luster. This is normal. If you look at your previous joy factor exercise, I bet there are still elements that are unchanging. At the same time, there will be elements that should be removed from your "today" list because they no longer bring the same level of excitement.

When you find that the negative elements out-weigh the positive and the honeymoon is over, it is time to refresh your self-assessment and determine where you stand. Complete your joy factor list and see what is exciting you and what is pulling you down. When you look at that list, if the negative side is comprised of elements that are environmental and not role-based, then you need to find a similar position but in a new company. For example: You love the job and its day-to-day responsibilities. But a difficult work environment like a bad boss or an unreasonable customer drains you. If the environment cannot be addressed, then it is time to move to a new job laterally.

If, in contrast, your list has changed on the substantive side of what you are doing and the once joyful elements are no longer bringing you excitement, then it is time to assess that change. Where can you find an opportunity that will continue to increase that side of the equation? I have found that if I have a good reputation and a good relationship with the leaders of an organization, these shifts can often happen within your current employer. I am a huge proponent of creating your own role versus hiring into a role someone else has defined. If you take the opportunity to work with your current employer, then it is much easier to get closer to your joy and create that perfect position. From an employer's perspective there is less risk with taking on a known entity. If you can demonstrate return on investment and how the organization will benefit, you will have an excellent chance of making it happen. Sometimes you can even start volunteering for elements of the new position and take on those responsibilities without making an official change.

For example, there was a time in my career when I was riding high and performing well from my employer's perspective. I knew that change was coming and the contract I was running was going to be competed for again and that would mean that I would have to commit for another year or elevate my successor into the role. So, I looked at what I loved about my current position. Many of the elements that I loved surrounded program management functions and working the system within my company. I had become very skilled at knowing how to get things accomplished within the firm.

I was not thrilled with my customer and how political the climate had become. An opportunity with an M&A (merger and acquisition) presented itself and an entire new group was coming into the company. The need to assimilate a large group of program managers into the firm, assess their skills, train them on how to get things accomplished, and provide oversight was required. I offered to mentor this group of individuals and train them on my company's methods and policies.

The company agreed and asked me to become the Deputy Division manager of that new Division. I got to exercise most of my joy list by helping those new PMs learn how to be effective at the firm and how to increase their effectiveness on their contracts. This new position was beyond rewarding. I eliminated all the factors that I detested and moved into a role that still had me exercising good PM acumen. It was a perfect transition. At the time I felt this is the perfect role for me. I was adding value, respected by the people I was helping and appreciated by the leadership team for the transformation that played out across this new division. What I didn't expect was the exposure to business development and portfolio financials. These were two things that I inherited from my past role, but never had to execute myself. So, here I was exercising my joy for most of my day and the rest I was learning new business areas that later would be added to my joy column.

This example is the perfect model of how to apply The Joy Factor assessment to your current situation to find a new job opportunity. Start with whatever company at which you are employed. As I said before, give your current employer the opportunity to provide you growth before looking outside the firm. In today's "no loyalty" environment, it is sometimes easier to move to the next situation externally, but I will tell you that it places you at a disadvantage from a momentum standpoint. If you have done well with a firm and have built your brand and reputation, then you often must start over when changing firms. It is an easier transition if you can accomplish the change internally. You are a known talent and that positive platform will follow you into that new role. A different firm will often require you to start over. So, again, it is in your best interest to let your current employer do the "right thing."

That doesn't mean you take a passive aggressive stance or a "Do for me or I go" attitude. You need to leverage your awareness of the needs of the firm and create an opportunity that matches your desire for change, your newly analyzed joy list, and the needs of the firm. You will be surprised how often your needs and the firm's needs match. And who better to identify that than you! Below is a table that looks at an issue a firm is having and how to leverage The Joy Factor to create opportunities for you.

Figure 5

Needs of Firm	Joy Factors	Proposal
10% of programs are losing money	Mentoring and coaching	Offer to work one-on-one with PM's that are struggling
10% of programs are losing money	Being the center of attention	Offer a "lunch & learn" on what levers a PM has to turn a struggling program around
10% of programs are losing money	Strategic thinking	Create get-well plan program or set of SOP's that the firm could use when programs fall into the "troubled" category

If you need to move to a new organization, the transition to a new company can be less scary when you have connections. If you make the decision to go, then start with firms that know your brand, strengths, and reputation. Then the "start from scratch" syndrome is less dramatic. Is there a customer you served or a partner in industry with whom you worked closely? Take inventory of your network, and when you decide to look externally, be sure to do so.

Having an advocate and mentor can help along the journey. Let's examine the role of a mentor. Mentors can be internal or external to your company. They can be formal or informal, just-in-time, or for a lifetime. I highly encourage you to have several mentors who you can use as advisors along your journey.

You will need someone who has insight into what is happening either in your company or out in the marketplace.

The transition I discussed above where I became a Deputy Division Manager, stemmed from a conversation I had with a formal mentor at my firm. She was deeply involved with the M&A and knew my superpowers could have a positive impact on the transition and save me from my current role. When selecting your mentor(s) be sure to find someone who has that influence and insight. Someone who will not only lift you up but will hold up a mirror from time to time. It is powerful to have a safe place to discuss your development and struggles. Good mentors can make those connections and find the puzzle pieces that will not necessarily be in your range of vision.

Summary

You and your joy factors will evolve. It's normal and expected. You can celebrate when you find a position that brings you contentment and enjoy all the aspects that provide fulfillment. Change is normal. Now you know how to handle that evolution. This is all a part of maturing into that dream position—the one that you can't really dream specifically about because it hasn't been defined yet.

Remember to be aware of the shifts and see if you can leverage your current employer to support your new interests and desires. It is in their best interest to help you along the way. Use the power of a mentor to help prepare the organization for what you will propose. Well-chosen mentors are very powerful in getting your goals accomplished.

Chapter 6

How to Accelerate Joy

Thus far, we have talked about two methods: changing your situation within your job and finding a new position externally. I personally have had great success when deploying the first method. Let's look at one of my favorite and most rewarding examples from my own career of creating a new role within your present company.

I lead the commercial cyber security program for a large federally based technology firm. At the time, the company was re-organizing again. An organization chart was released, and I immediately noticed that my current division was divided up and re-assigned to new Division Managers. I also quickly noticed that I was not on the chart at all. When I asked my boss if I should look for a new opportunity, he quickly apologized and let me know that they had a special assignment for me. This new role would be bringing together several commercial cyber practices for the first time, in an attempt to legitimize the company's cyber offering.

I immediately got excited. This new role would combine some elements of my joy factor list that I previously thought I wouldn't get to exercise— mainly the entrepreneurial and team-building side. This was like starting a new business, and there were commercial elements that just weren't available in the company. I would get to establish elements like hiring commissioned based sales force and establishing channel relationships from scratch. The business was in the red at the time. Working through how to become profitable and not deteriorate the service was a huge challenge that I really enjoyed.

This was an opportunity to accelerate joy factors that I didn't think I would get to experience for many years. This also represented doing something I had never done before. At the time I didn't know if cyber security was spelled as one word or two (this is a joke, as it can be both). I was nervous because I was asked to lead a team that I didn't really know the acumen of what we were delivering. What I did know is that I had owned two prior companies, and I knew how to take dysfunctional teams and get them to work as one. I leaned on those strengths and didn't try to hide what I didn't know. Once again, I was exercising a core joy element for me, just like sign language interpreting, in which I needed to learn something brand new. Like my previous experience, I jumped in with both feet, read a lot of materials, asked a ton of questions, and leaned on my leadership team. I watched, took note of their hot buttons, and learned the business.

Take a detailed look at that list we created together a few chapters back. What can you do in your current positions to make subtle shifts that could dramatically increase your joy? What items on the list can I control and what items must I live with? Indicate which items you can focus on and adjust or change for your benefit.

Figure 6

Joy Tasks	Negative Tasks
Mentoring others	Approving requisitions
Coaching a team through a difficult problem	Telling someone they need to improve their work products*
Productive meetings	Super long meetings where nothing was decided*
Winning a proposal	Organizing your desk*
Proofreading oth-ers' work	Writing that first paragraph of a long executive summary*
Motivating others to take on something new	Running out of things to do*

There are things on this list that I can totally control. As you can see, I put an asterisk next to each negative joy factor that I could do something about such as organizing my desk. There are systems I could put in place on organization and filing schemes, etc. that would minimize the disorganization. There are probably ten thousand self-help books on this topic alone.

How can you accelerate The Joy Factor elements? You will be surprised how just asking yourself that question will reveal solutions. Is there additional work for which you can volunteer to take off your co-workers' plates? Are there adjacent departments that you could volunteer to take on some of their workload to give you the experience, or simply to do more of the work in

The Joy Factor column? You may need to work more than you do today to get to do what you want. You will notice that when you start working from a place of pure joy, the day will fly by, you won't notice that eight hours in the day have passed. When you start working for yourself in that way, then how you define your hours and the time becomes yours not the company's.

The exposure and experiences you can gain by looking beyond the square box will fulfill you and you will enjoy it, but more importantly your definition of your role will grow. Then you get to have more joy to document on your resume. This is how you create your own joy.

Be sure you find out the expectations of your new position. If you were hired for that square box

and there are components of what
you must do that you do not love,
then accentuate the positive and
make sure the quality of everything
you do is good. As Mark Twain
said, "Eat the frog!" In other words,
do the hardest, yuckiest tasks, and
do them first so you can move on to
the rest of your day with joy. This
is like when you were a kid and
you ate your broccoli before you
ate your macaroni and cheese. I am
advocating following your passion
without getting fired.

The second way to accelerate
your joy is to find a new position
that has an environment that will allow your joy to grow. It is true that
the best time to find a new position
is when you don't have to locate
one. Finding a new position is best
when your job search is driven by

joy instead of resentment.

Use your journal and joy list to determine the type of new position that will satisfy more of the joy factors and how you will grow in the role. Take inventory of the skills you think you need to give you credentials to do more of what you like. For example, if you have gone to school to be a teacher, and you have worked several years being an elementary school teacher, then your joy list looks something like this table below.

Figure 7

Joy Factors	Negatives
Teaching	Short attention span of age group
Lesson-planning	Large classrooms
Interacting with parents	Not enough supplies to properly educate
Teaching Math & Science	Uncompensated hours
PTA	Disciplining
Changing lives	

Now what you need to do is take this list and see if there are elements that you are not currently doing that you could be learning. Include those elements even if you haven't tried them before. To answer the growth element, include capabilities or tasks that you don't have that you will need to learn for that new position. Match them with transition activities or experiences that you can do now to help prepare you for that next role.

Figure 8

Joy Factors	Negatives
Teaching	Short attention span of age group
Lesson-planning	Large classrooms
Interacting with parents	Not enough supplies to properly educate
Teaching math & science	Uncompensated v hours
PTA	Disciplining
Changing lives	

+

Future Joy Factors	Transition Opportunities
Teaching at a middle school	Lead the Math Club
Learning to teach upper-level math courses	Tutor middle school aged kids in math and science

Summary

Just do it! Incorporate activities that allow you to experience more assignments that you like and that will allow you to grow your calling. Often the easiest place to do that is to look for opportunities where you are currently employed. Leverage your brand, your hard work, and your goodwill to negotiate for opportunities and additional experiences in the areas that you have targeted. Should you need to look elsewhere, make sure you are clear on your objectives and have a solid understanding of what the next position requires, so you are not stuck in the same role. Remember: it's not the job title but The Joy Factor that leads you to where you need to be.

Chapter 7

Fab Five

....

What are you branding? So you have done the work. You have narrowed down your joy factors and can clearly articulate what it is you want. That is a powerful position to be in. Most people are very good at describing, complaining, and whining about what they don't want to do. The conversation takes on more credibility and power when you are campaigning for your joy. When you describe how you want to help the firm by leveraging your superpowers, then the task begin to feed your passion. If you are a squeaky wheel, then you will not gain supporters for your cause. However, being someone who volunteers to take on more in the areas that you love is interpreted in a totally different light.

If you are looking for a new position, then make sure you represent what you want on your resume. I have noticed when reviewing resumes for people who are frustrated with their current position and are looking for change, that there is no sign that they want something different. What they have documented in their resume brands them for more of the same misery.

When documenting your experience, be sure to dig out The Joy Factor list to rewrite your history! I'm not saying, "Make things up"— that would be dishonest. What I am saying is, this is a chance to tell a different story about your journey for joy. The journal that you have created is your resume. Talk about the assignments, awards, and major projects that brought you joy. Your objective/summary section at the top should lead the reader to your next position that will increase the opportunity for more passion. People often make the mistake of documenting the things they detest in their resume and attract more of the same when looking for the next opportunity, so don't make that mistake!

Let's take a look: This was the journal that we created in the third chapter.

Figure 9

Position	Positives	Negatives	Lessons
C++ Maintenance Programmer	The win in solving the bugs, talking to the end users, sharing what I learned	Solitude, working alone, staring at someone else's code, the wins are too far apart	I like to solve hard problems, be with people, I don't have the patience to figure out programming problems
Sign Language Interpreter	Being the center of attention, learning how to own a business, the challenge of learning a new language and culture	Interpreters cannot give their opinion; they can't solve problems when they are interpreting	I love the attention, the challenge of learning something new and the business elements, but I also love to give my opinion
Technical Trainer	Being the center of attention, public speaking, helping others learn	Teach the same thing over and over	I still love the attention, but I do not like doing the same thing everyday, repetition
ISP Co-Owner	Loved setting up the business, watching the business grow, accounts receivable, budgeting, marketing	Losing bids, solitude	I learned that I loved finance and business growth and marketing, I enjoy an office with more people than less

You can easily take the first two columns to be entries into your resume. Let's take the first one in the list and show how you can document this experience in two different ways.

Traditional Example

Company ABC/Computer Programmer: *Performed maintenance programming using C++ on a Unix platform for a complicated custom application. Solved discrepancy reports and documented code changes.*

Joy Example

Company ABC/Computer Programmer: *Served as the customer liaison in investigating technical issues that were impacting performance. Validated that mitigation strategies and code changes, in C++ were effective and solved the customer's performance issues. Through maintenance enhancements and error corrections was able to discover process improvements that increased customer efficiencies. Instructed technical personnel on lessons learned and documented the results for future use.*

In the Joy example I am painting a picture about how I really like working with customers. You really can't determine if I was doing maintenance programming. Remember, I hated maintenance programming. The Joy example demonstrates that I had an acumen for it while highlighting my skills in customer services and teaching within the company.

Take an honest look at the

front page of your resume. What story does it tell? It should paint a very clear picture of what you are looking to do next. Again, your objective/summary should directly tell the reader what kind of position you seek. You may have won your company's top performance award for something you hated doing. Don't celebrate that on the first page and be very careful of what you are trying to convey. Remember your resume must be accurate and it needs to market you.

Let's explore your internal brand. For what are you famous in your current employment? Is your brand a positive or negative one? You need to have a plan to market yourself internally. It is easy for the people on your team or group to know who you are, but building a brand that will provide you leverage requires marketing your work beyond your current group or team.

How do you do that? You might say, "Hey, I'm hired to do job X yet job X only lets me work with my current group and I believe I can help the company grow by extending out more." You must have situational awareness and be a good networker. On the day-to-day job front look for any opportunity to work with adjacent teams. Then of course you need to knock it out of the park! Do a great job and make an impression. Go above and beyond and don't forget the power of a compliment and a thank you. When the interaction is complete, send a thank you email or complimentary message for the folks who are not in your normal circle. Make sure they remember you.

Beyond your day-to-day activities the opportunities to network are plentiful and unlimited. Network where you have real interest. Large companies will have a variety of opportunities. Some examples include social activities like corporate sport events, picnics, or holiday parties. Philanthropic opportunities that are corporately sponsored are another good way. There are often relationship groups for emerging professionals, members of the military, or women's groups in which you can participate and add value. Technical or discipline-oriented groups are another excellent way to network.

Participating at these events or with these groups will help you build initial relationships. To really make your mark and take it up a level, I recommend volunteering within those groups to help organize an event or even lead one of them. Offering to help or raising your hand is such a simple and easy way to get involved.

For example, when I was running that super large program, the team earned our first 100 percent award fee. Soon after the award, I offered to give a presentation and share our strategy on how to prepare and convince your customer to give you perfect marks. The corporate Program Management Forum eagerly agreed to have me be a guest speaker. I went from being one person in a large group sitting in the audience to speaking to that group. Six months later I was asked to be the Chairperson for the Program Management Forum! One of

the benefits of being the chairperson was a bi-annual meeting with
the CEO of the company. For a 10
billion-dollar company, getting the
opportunity to make that impression
was priceless. That transition from
being a member of the audience to
briefing the CEO took less than six
months.

Now let's discuss the power
of a genuine compliment. You can
manage your own brand and boost
the effectiveness of your self-mar-
keting when you connect with others through a genuine compliment.
Once I was attending a leadership
event with hundreds of people at the
session. One of the speakers was a
President of the company (we had
four Presidents at that level), and
she was reviewing her group with
the help of an organizational chart

during a briefing. I noticed that there were many women on the organizational chart, and it resonated with me. So, I didn't keep it to myself. The next day I sent her an email and complimented her for "walking the talk" in promoting women in a very male dominated company. I ended the note with an offer to take her to lunch someday, so I could pick her brain and learn how she was successful in creating such a diverse organization.

That afternoon she had her administrative assistant schedule a private meeting and we spent several hours getting to know each other. We had much in common and our shared experiences helped to create a bond. It didn't end there: the next week, she shared our experience with the President that oversaw my group, which influenced him to want to meet me. After spending time with him, we established a formal mentoring relationship that lasted for many years. Even today we follow each other's careers and congratulate each other's successes. I would use our time together to share success stories about our program, teams, and customers' accomplishments. He would then share those stories in very public forums. That mentoring relationship was critical to building my brand.

An enjoyable way to maintain your network is by having dinner with peers, and for me it is a group of ladies, all powerful and accomplished in their own ways. We call ourselves the Fabulous Five (or the Fab Five for short)! We meet for dinner five or six times a year to celebrate our accomplishments, learn about market trends, and share ideas. We are like Napoleon Hill's "mastermind group" in his famous 1925 book, The Law of Success.). The truth is, we genuinely enjoy our time together and often will move appointments (even a business trip once) to not miss our gathering. So yes, networking can be natural and can be fun. If any member of the Fab Five was in trouble or needed help in any way I know without a doubt we would all come rushing in to help the other.

Lastly, don't forget that your co-workers and peers you work with every day are a source for brand expansion. You know each other and have great rapport. If these people are positive influences in your life and you have a mutual respect, then put energy and effort into the relationship. Linked-in and other forms of social media are a great way to maintain an awareness of what people are doing. Make an effort to stay connected. It can be as simple as having coffee or lunch a few times a year.

Summary

Your brand is something that takes thoughtful consideration and focus to develop and nurture. How others and the organization perceive you can have a positive influence on your career and can follow you from position to position and from company to company. The adage to not burn bridges still holds true today. There is an element of being genuine that is critical in all this. Find the experience that you enjoy or areas where you are trying to learn and create opportunities to develop that brand. How you market yourself is totally in your control. It is reflected in your resume, in your networking, and in how you stay connected to the colleagues that you treasure the most.

Chapter 8

It All Works Out In the End

So many people make the mistake of moving to a new position for financial reasons only. They take on more duties that do not fall into the "joy" category for the improved income. They work in these positions and continue to build the wrong brand. Their credentials do not grow towards their joy, but away from it.

A story about Karma and money. I took seven years off to raise my children. When coming back to the workforce it was a scary proposition, but I didn't realize that

I had this weapon called hunger and eagerness. There was an experience that I will never forget, an interview that is vividly imprinted in my brain. It was with a small company and the interview was with the President of the company. I arrived respectably 15 minutes early. Then I waited, and I waited. I was finally called into this very messy office. Piles of papers and books everywhere. He waived me into the office and pointed to a chair as he was finishing a phone call. So, I sat there listening for what felt like an eternity as he completed his call. Finally, he hung up and sighed. He looked at me and said, "You present yourself well, but with your gap in service I don't think I can even get you in front of my customer." Wow, what an opening, I was shocked that the guy even wasted his and my time by having me come to the interview. I told him that we should probably part ways and I wished him luck with his business.

A few weeks later I interviewed with a very large company and the woman who met with me recognized my entrepreneurial experience and even the charitable organizations that I ran while I was a stay-at-home mom. At the interview she said that not only would she like to hire me, but that I seemed to have the organizational skills to run one of their largest programs. I told her that I would love to come work for her and the company. She asked about compensation. I told her that I knew that from a market perspective where I thought I should be, but recognized she was taking a risk with someone who had had such a long break. I told her to offer me 20 percent less than the market rate and if I proved myself in a year's time then she should increase my salary.

For the next three years I received double-digit percentage increases and was promoted three times into that large program that she had mentioned in the interview. I more than doubled my salary and I was getting bonuses with stocks, options, and cash. I even received a grant, retention bonus that would mature in five years to get me to stay. I had never made so much money in my life. Moreover, these opportunities came with leadership activities that I loved doing. I was now collecting an enormous salary to do them.

Now for the Karma: This very large program I was running for the

company had over 70 subcontract-
ing companies working on it. One
of those sub-contracting companies
earned 90 percent of their revenue
through my vehicle. You guessed it:
it was none other than that disorga-
nized, rude President that wouldn't
give me the time of day. I would
host status meetings with our sub-
contractors and he always made a
point to grovel in his own way. This
is also a lesson in the golden rule.
You should always treat all people
with respect. You never know who
might hold your fate or the things
you care about in their control.

It truly was a "turn the page"
situation, and a totally different
reality. Going from being humiliat-
ed in an interview and questioning
my own personal worth to being on
top, running one of the largest pro-

grams within my company, win-
ning awards, and having someone
who once dismissed me, now eating
humble pie. That alone can be satis-
fying, but when I look back, it was
the courage: the internal strength to
not let a negative experience feed my
insecurities.

When you follow your dreams
and passions the rest will fall into
place. That is what all the famous
successful people say. I know you
are probably thinking the same thing
I once thought: "Easy for them to
state since they have already made
it." They have their riches and fame.
It is easy to tell others that they can
have it all when you are sitting on
top. I am here to tell you that, from
a career perspective, you can have
it all, but it takes work and it takes
courage. Courage to sometimes not

take that new, shiny position for money's sake, but to take the path less traveled: your path. When you follow that joy, you tend to work harder and drive to be the best. I promise you that the compensation will come.

For me, the money came, and it came quickly. When I started that first company to escape the programming job I hated, and I wasn't worried about money. In fact, I would make lists of things to do that included minimizing expenses and looking for other ways to supplement the transition. With $30,000 annually, I was making great money for a college graduate in 1989. That was way more than my friends were able to get and there was this fear that I would never be able to make that much money doing something different. Boy, was I wrong.

In less than a year of moving forward with my dream to own my own company, I had more than doubled my income! I was pursuing my passion and taking the steps required to do so like incorporating, getting insurance, getting certified, establishing a sole source contract with the government, and all these steps were so exciting! The following through with these new tasks and escaped the misery of programming. I was running to my dream and it was so thrilling that I didn't worry about the money. It came, and more than provided.

Following my passion and joy was not always a journey I traveled with full abandon. There were times when I would take "safe" routes. I chose a position that I could "fall back on," knowing I could perform, but also knowing I wouldn't love it. When I went back to work after taking off with my kids it was scary, and I knew I could be a Systems Integrator, using my management skills and my IT background to manage technology-oriented projects. I just wanted to get my foot in the door. I was not following my passion.

Once in the position something happened. The customer leadership crumbled, we had a major delivery to bring to the community and all the stakeholders were fighting. Plus, at the same time the organization announced they wanted the team of 30 developers with which I was working to physically move to a new location. No one was in charge, so I just volunteered. I offered to help coordinate the move and took the steps to make this major transition be successful.

More importantly, I took over the meetings with the stakeholders and righted the ship so we could deliver the system and meet the expectation of providing a new capability that at the time was critical for the customer's mission. The customer went to my management and they promoted me to Contract Program Manager for the program. This was a huge honor, as normally the customer liked to maintain control of that position. It is not often that a customer requests that their vendor change someone's position and offer them more compensation. In this case, although the initial position of Systems Integrator was taken due to fear, I made the best of the opportunities while in the role. I volunteered to take on tasks I loved doing, including organization and program management. Rather than asking for a raise or a new title, I received a raise due to the work and effort that I put in. The money came soon after and so did the title.

Summary

It will always require more than you think is necessary to expand your horizons. Yet, when you do more, you will gain more when you least expect it. I did not know how successfully I would flourish while serving as a Systems Integrator. Nor did I know that I would be managing the work of the company head that disrespected me during a job interview. My sole focus was on maximizing my potential and expanding upon the joy factors within the position that I held at the time. I took risks for lower than expected pay with the knowledge that if I worked hard, I would be rewarded for my efforts at a later time. If you actualize The Joy Factor, then it will truly work out in the end.

Chapter 9

The Courage and the Discipline to Start

It can be very unnerving to even contemplate making a move. In reality, this is an exciting journey. Just thinking about next steps to move to a happier place can be motivation enough to progress forward. If it isn't, then take some time to figure out what is holding you back. For many, it is the power of the unknown. To help demystify some of the unknown and give you power back, write the possibilities down. Make an inventory of all the risks associated with making a big move. Sometimes just seeing that list will take away some of its power and hold you accountable. Here is a hypothetical example of a move from a bookkeeping position to becoming a chef.

Figure 10

Risks
Loss of income
Not enough cooking experience
Change in health insurance coverage
New hours

Your list can be as long as you need to feel like you have captured all the reasons why this could fail. Now review the list and see if it still is as bad as it seems now that you have it all in one place. The next step is to take control and calm yourself as you document how you will mitigate each risk.

Figure 11

Risks	Mitigation Plan
Loss of income	Research going rates for salaries and move to smaller housing if required, reduce expenses
Not enough cooking experience	Look into culinary schools
Change in health insurance coverage	Find a full-time position that offers coverage, research the price of coverage and know what those costs are upfront
New hours	Next vacation take a week and stay up late at night being very productive and sleep in late to see how it feels

Whoa...wait a minute. This list has me potentially moving to a smaller house! YES! When pursuing your chance to be happy, it might mean taking a step back initially to have the opportunity to live your dream. Sometimes tests like this are true gut checking moments where you can decide if being happy is worth it. Are you truly committed, have you burned your boats, as Sun Tzu (Tzu, 5th Century) would ask?

Also look at the list again. Once you have a mitigation plan documented, then you can start working at each risk and fear until you have gained confidence in your ability to control and overcome each one! You get your power back.

When developing your mitigation plans, ask for help. Ask people who are in the industry or position you would like to have, how they have navigated each risk. Having a plan and having it validated will increase your confidence and make your next steps easier to take. Plus, these mitigation plans often turn into transition plans or roadmaps on how to get there. Ask your mentor or people you trust to give you input on your list. Are you missing anything, have you left something off?

You don't want to put all your energy on the negative list. I want you to spend even more time on the positive side. Now comes the fun part. You get to imagine with as much detail as you can muster the ways that you will describe your new position, especially the benefits side. What will be fun? What will you learn? Imagine how this new position will be rewarding and how your days will fly by! Create this new list, an aspirational list that details your new activities. You will be able to feel the joy prior to making the move. Then you know you are ready.

By the way, mistakes are bound to happen. We all make mistakes. It's normal. It's okay. How you handle the mistakes, defines how you will evolve from them. Always be open to the possibility, the real possibility, that you are wrong, flawed, not perfect, and that you and those affected by your work would be better off if you had made a different decision.

When you come to that understanding, that you made some type of error, it is critical to manage it. Be transparent, ask for forgiveness and own the cleanup. If you take these steps, you might even make out better than if you had made the right decision and not made a mistake.

When interviewing for that large Program Management position, the one that truly defined my career, I made a terrible mistake. When the position was brought to my attention, I had just come off from being the hero on that program that lost its customer's leadership team. I was flying high and was recognized internally and externally for the value that I brought to the organization. I was given advice from my mentor, that going through the interview process for this position would be a good experience and that I could learn from the process. I shouldn't worry too much as over 50 people had applied for the position. So, I applied.

The process started with a panel of five individuals asking a series of specific questions about the program. I was doing quite well when they asked me a very technical question that was specific to the program and I didn't have a clue what they were asking. I started to stumble and try to "fake" an answer to the question I didn't understand. Halfway through my response, I stopped. I stopped talking and paused. The silence was uncomfortable for everyone in the room. I knew I didn't understand and decided I needed to stop rambling. I looked at the person who asked me the question and said, "I don't think I understand your question, I'm sorry, but what I have responded with so far, I believe is not right. Can you explain your question differently?" The interviewer re-stated the question differently with more explana-

tions and then I immediately under-
stood and took the time to respond
thoroughly with a more than appro-
priate response.

After the panel interviews
and a four-part series of individual
interviews, I got the position. When
talking to my boss later, she stated,
"You know, you were like Nancy
Kerrigan, you fell right on your ass,
but got back up and delivered the
triple axel". (Nancy Kerrigan is a
famous Figure Skater who competed
in the Olympics in 1991 and 1993).
It's not about failing. Rather, it's
about how we get back up with humility, honesty, and a genuine desire
to finish strong.

Summary

Jump in, do it, get started. Create

your lists and mitigation measures. Validate your analysis and ask for support. It's okay to fail. But you must be vigilant about recovering well from mistakes with honesty, humility, and renewed hard work. The most important lesson is to reveal the value that you bring to your work. When it's time to move, move with courage and know that the preparations and hard work that you executed on your current job will serve as a calling card for recognition in the next role within your career.

Afterword

Finding joy is a personal experience that can only be defined and experienced by you. It is an individual journey that requires you to be honest with yourself, do the work, and not be afraid to take the first steps.

I encourage you take quality time with your journals, and remember most people don't know what they want to be when they grow up! It is normal and okay to have a journey that starts on one path and changes. That is a strong indication that you are growing and learning. Time is not wasted. It is there for us to test ourselves. Take account of our strengths, gifts, and how we want to walk through life.

Have an anchor, be grateful

and most importantly be aware. Be present for your own journey. Remember the law of attraction and creating a positive environment that will be the foundation for success.

Remember to foster your brand and market your joy factors. Don't forget to make clear the value you add to the organization so others can support your pursuits. Make it easy for people to know what you love to do so they can support you.

Figure 12

Joy Factor Steps

☐   Frame your mind for joy and gratitude

☐   Create your Joy Factor list

☐   Apply weighting percentages to each factor

☐   Create Job Journal with Lessons Learned

☐   Identify skills to develop and experience
     required for transitions

☐   Make changes at your current job so you can
     Brand them and who you are most efficiently

☐   Match the needs of the firm with opportuni-
     ties for Joy

☐   Do it – get started!!

Don't deviate from your joy

Let it guide you, inspire you, and provide for you.

Thank you for reading to the end and listening to all my stories!

Now go do it!

ISBN 978-1-7342893-5-0

aspirebooks.org

Made in the USA
Lexington, KY
27 November 2019